SUPER SIMPLE
ENGINEERING PROJECTS

ENGINEER IT!
BRIDGE
PROJECTS

CAROLYN BERNHARDT

CONSULTING EDITOR, DIANE CRAIG, M.A./READING SPECIALIST

Super Sandcastle

An Imprint of Abdo Publishing
abdopublishing.com

abdopublishing.com

Published by Abdo Publishing, a division of ABDO, PO Box 398166, Minneapolis, Minnesota 55439. Copyright © 2018 by Abdo Consulting Group, Inc. International copyrights reserved in all countries. No part of this book may be reproduced in any form without written permission from the publisher. Super SandCastle™ is a trademark and logo of Abdo Publishing.

Printed in the United States of America, North Mankato, Minnesota
062017
092017

THIS BOOK CONTAINS
RECYCLED MATERIALS

Production: Mighty Media, Inc.
Editor: Liz Salzmann
Cover Photographs: Mighty Media, Inc.; Shutterstock
Interior Photographs: iStockphoto; Mighty Media, Inc.; Shutterstock

The following manufacturers/names appearing in this book are trademarks: Aleene's® Tacky Glue®, Elmer's® Glue-All™, Pyrex®, Sharpie®

Publisher's Cataloging-in-Publication Data

Names: Bernhardt, Carolyn, author.
Title: Engineer it! bridge projects / by Carolyn Bernhardt.
Other titles: Bridge projects
Description: Minneapolis, MN : Abdo Publishing, 2018. | Series: Super simple engineering projects
Identifiers: LCCN 2016963076 | ISBN 9781532111228 (lib. bdg.) | ISBN 9781680789072 (ebook)
Subjects: LCSH: Bridges--Juvenile literature. | Bridges--Design and construction--Juvenile literature. | Civil engineering--Juvenile literature.
Classification: DDC 624--dc23
LC record available at http://lccn.loc.gov/2016963076

Super SandCastle™ books are created by a team of professional educators, reading specialists, and content developers around five essential components—phonemic awareness, phonics, vocabulary, text comprehension, and fluency—to assist young readers as they develop reading skills and strategies and increase their general knowledge. All books are written, reviewed, and leveled for guided reading and early reading intervention programs for use in shared, guided, and independent reading and writing activities to support a balanced approach to literacy instruction.

TO ADULT HELPERS

The projects in this title are fun and simple. There are just a few things to remember. Some projects require the use of hot objects. Also, kids may be using messy materials such as glue or paint. Make sure they protect their clothes and work surfaces. Review the projects before starting, and be ready to assist when necessary.

KEY SYMBOL

Watch for this warning symbol in this book. Here is what it means.

HOT!
You will be working with something hot. Get help!

CONTENTS

WHAT IS A
BRIDGE?

A bridge is a structure that crosses over something. Bridges allow people to go over **obstacles**. This makes travel faster and safer.

Many bridges cross bodies of water, such as rivers. Bridges also connect islands to **mainlands**.

Other bridges are built over obstacles on land. For example, many highways have bridges that let roads cross over each other. These are called overpasses.

BRIDGE OVER WATER

HIGHWAY OVERPASS

PARTS OF A BRIDGE

There are many kinds of bridges. They all look a little different. But there are a few basic parts that are similar in all bridges. The surface of a bridge is called the bridge deck. The bridge deck has at least two supports. The part of a support that is above ground is a pier. The part that is below ground is a pile. A place where an end of the bridge deck meets a support is called an abutment. The section of bridge deck between two piers is called a span. A bridge can have one or many spans.

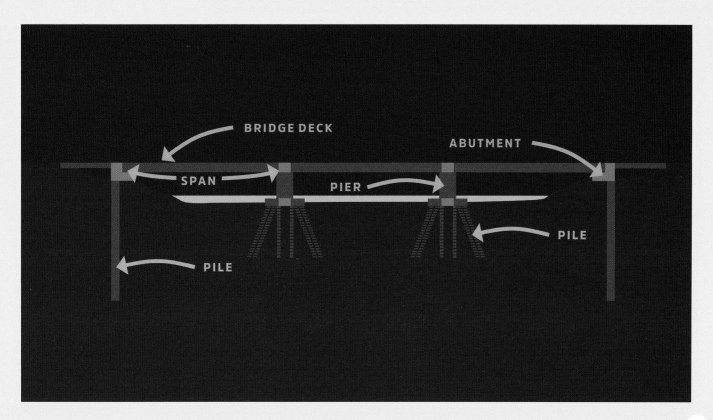

HOW PEOPLE
USE BRIDGES

Bridges are built for different kinds of **traffic**. These include bicycles and **pedestrians**, trains, and cars. Some bridges have sections for two or more types of traffic.

FOOT TRAFFIC

People walk across the Millennium Bridge in London, England.

THE GOLDEN GATE BRIDGE

The Golden Gate Bridge is in California. It connects the city of San Francisco and Marin County. The bridge opened in 1937. It is one of the most famous bridges in the world. It has six lanes for car **traffic**. It also has pathways for **pedestrians** and bicycles. Every day, more than 100,000 people cross the Golden Gate Bridge.

CAR TRAVEL

Cars drive across the San Francisco–Oakland Bay Bridge in California.

TRAIN CONNECTIONS

A train crosses the New River in West Virginia.

TYPES OF
BRIDGES

There are six main types of bridges. They are suspension, arch, cable-stayed, cantilever, beam, and truss.

SUSPENSION

A suspension bridge hangs from large cables connected to towers. Smaller cables connect the large cables to the bridge deck.

ARCH

An arch bridge uses an arch to push the bridge's weight toward its ends. Some arch bridges have more than one arch.

CABLE-STAYED

A cable-stayed bridge hangs from cables. All of the cables are connected to the bridge's towers.

CANTILEVER

A cantilever bridge has two spans that meet in the middle. Each span has its own support.

BEAM

A beam bridge is the simplest kind of bridge. It is a flat surface resting on supports.

TRUSS

A truss bridge has support beams arranged in triangles. The beams make the bridge extra strong.

MATERIALS

Here are some of the materials that you will need for the projects in this book.

 **BLACK TAPE**

 **BOOKS**

 **CARDBOARD**

 **CLAY**

 **CORRECTION TAPE**

 **CRAFT GLUE**

 **DRINKING STRAWS**

 **HOLE PUNCH**

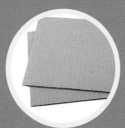 **MARBLES**

 **MARKERS**

 **MEASURING CUP**

 **MEDIUM-SIZED BOWL**

NEEDLE-NOSE PLIERS

NEWSPAPER

PAINT

PAINTBRUSHES

PAPER CLIPS

PENNIES

PENS

PLASTIC CUP

RAMEKIN

RULER

SCISSORS

SCREW EYES

SMALL TIN BOX

SQUARE TISSUE BOX

STRAIGHT PINS

THIN COPPER WIRE

WOODEN CRAFT STICKS

WRAPPING-PAPER TUBE

CABLE-STAYED
BRIDGE

MATERIALS: 2 wrapping-paper tubes, ruler, marker, scissors, cardboard, newspaper, paint (black and another color), paintbrush, correction tape, hole punch, 6 screw eyes, thin copper wire, black tape, toy cars and trucks

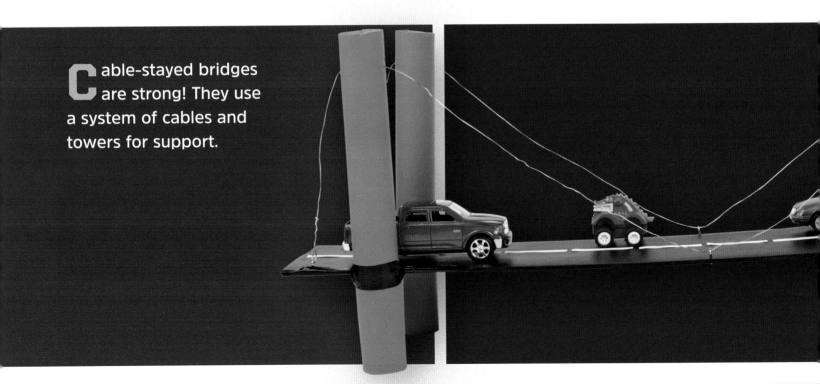

Cable-stayed bridges are strong! They use a system of cables and towers for support.

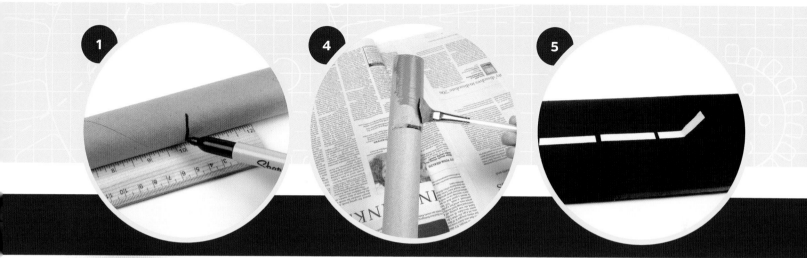

1 Make a mark 10 inches (25 cm) from the end of a tube. Cut the tube at the mark. Repeat to cut three more tube pieces.

2 Make a mark 3 inches (7.5 cm) from one end of each tube piece. Cut a **slit** at each mark. Only cut halfway through the tubes.

3 Cut a strip of cardboard 5 by 24 inches (13 by 60 cm). This is the bridge deck.

4 Paint the bridge deck black. Paint the tubes any color you choose. Let the paint dry.

5 Use correction tape to make a lane line down the middle of the bridge deck.

Continued on the next page.

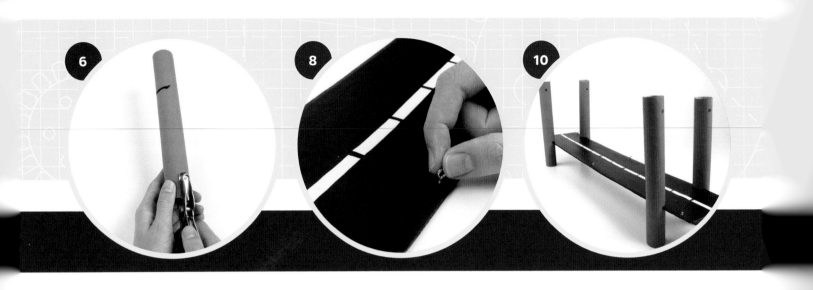

CABLE-STAYED BRIDGE (CONTINUED)

6 Punch a hole 1 inch (2.5 cm) from the end of a tube farthest from the **slit**. The hole should be even with one end of the slit. Punch another hole on the opposite side of the tube.

7 Repeat step 6 to punch two holes in each of the other tubes.

8 Measure 12 inches (30 cm) from one end of the bridge deck. Twist a screw eye into each side of the bridge deck at that point.

9 Twist a screw eye into each corner of the bridge deck about 1 inch (2.5 cm) from the end.

10 Slide the bridge deck into the slits in the tubes. Place a tube on each side of the bridge deck about 2 inches (5 cm) from the end.

11 Cut two pieces of wire. Make them each about 40 inches (100 cm) long.

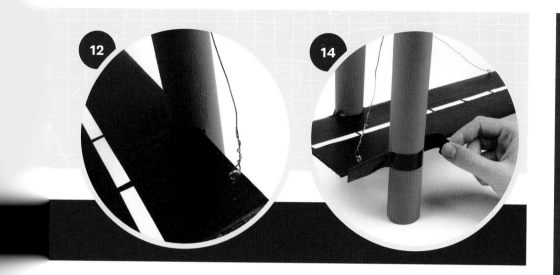

12 Wrap one end of a wire through a corner screw eye. Thread the other end through the holes in the top of the nearest tube. Then thread the wire through the middle screw eye on that side and then through the top of the tube on the other end. Finally, wrap the end through the screw eye in the nearest corner.

⑬ Repeat step 12 with the other wire on the other side of the bridge deck.

14 Use tape to help secure the tubes to the bridge deck.

⑮ Add cars and trucks driving across the bridge. Does the bridge stand up well under the weight?

DIGGING DEEPER

Most cable-stayed bridges have many cables on each side. Each cable supports a small area of the bridge deck. Together, they can hold more weight than just one cable could. The weight of the bridge pulls down on the cables. The cables **transfer** the weight to the towers. The bases of the towers are sunk deep underground. This helps the towers support the bridge.

STICK ARCH
BRIDGE

MATERIALS: water, measuring cup, microwave oven, medium-sized bowl, 20 long wooden craft sticks, 4 ramekins, scissors, cardboard, craft glue, about 40 short wooden craft sticks, pen, ruler, large book, toy train

The ancient Greeks built the first arch bridges more than 3,000 years ago. But the ancient Romans later perfected the arch bridge. They built hundreds of arch bridges in more than 20 countries. Many of these bridges are still used today.

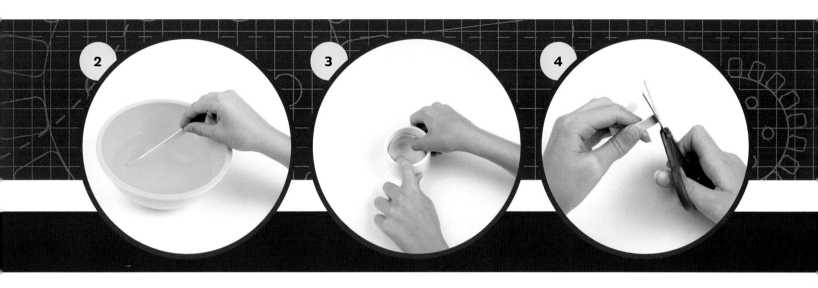

¹ Boil 3 cups (0.7 L) of water in a microwave oven. Carefully pour the hot water into a bowl.

² Put eight long craft sticks in the bowl. Leave them in the water for 5 minutes.

³ Remove the craft sticks from the bowl. Gently bend each stick to fit into a ramekin. Put two sticks in each ramekin. Let the sticks dry overnight.

⁴ Carefully remove the sticks from the ramekins. Trim the ends of the sticks to flatten them. These are the arches for the bridge.

Continued on the next page.

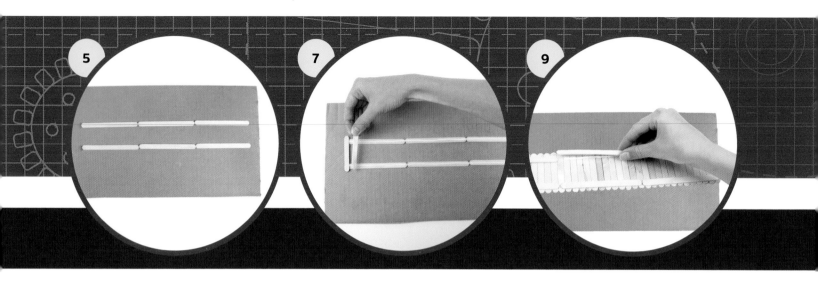

STICK ARCH BRIDGE (CONTINUED)

5 Make two straight rows of three long craft sticks. Line the sticks up end to end on the cardboard.

6 Put a line of glue on each row of sticks.

7 Place short craft sticks across the rows. Make sure they are right next to each other.

8 Add more sticks until the long sticks are covered. Be sure to place a short craft stick across each place the long craft sticks meet. Let the glue dry. This is the bridge deck.

9 Turn the bridge deck over. Glue long craft sticks along both edges. Let the glue dry.

10 Trace around the bridge deck on the cardboard. Set the bridge deck aside.

11 Draw a line along each long side of the traced shape. Draw each line ¼ inch (0.5 cm) in from the edge.

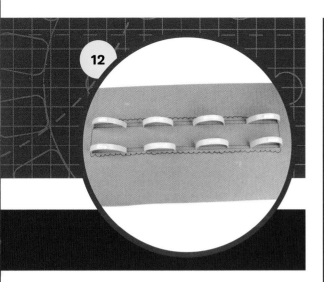

12 Place the arches inside the straight lines. Space them evenly. Put glue on top of each arch.

13 Place the bridge deck on top of the arches. Set a book on the bridge to press the deck into the arches. Let the glue dry.

14 Remove the book. Push the toy train across your arch bridge!

DIGGING DEEPER

Load is the weight supported by a bridge. In an arch bridge, the arch directs the load along the curve to the ends. This force is called compression. The Romans built their arch bridges out of stone. Compression causes each stone to press tightly against the stone next to it. This holds the bridge in place.

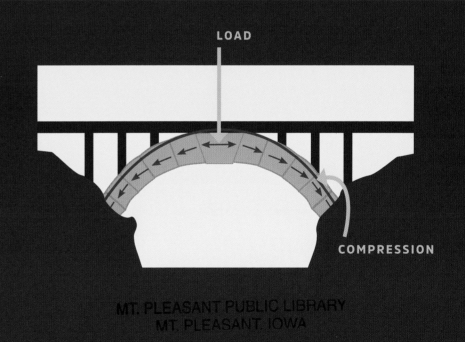

LOAD

COMPRESSION

BENDY BEAM
BRIDGE

MATERIALS: 30 straight drinking straws, scissors, ruler, marker, cardboard, 80 straight pins, needle-nose pliers, 2 square tissue boxes, plastic cup, marbles

A beam bridge has a support at each end. Weight on the bridge causes the bridge to bend. Engineers have to know how much weight a bridge needs to hold before building it.

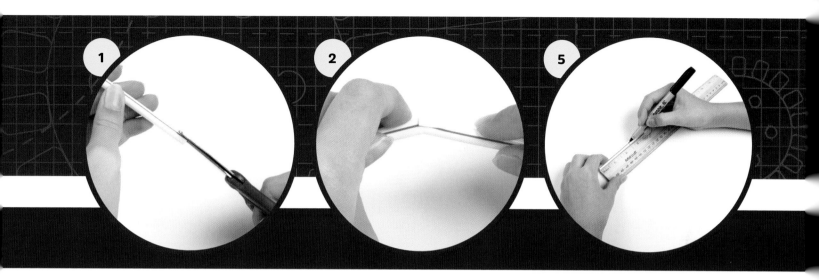

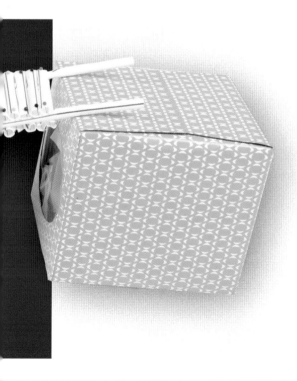

1. Cut a **slit** in one end of a straw.

2. Pinch the cut end of the straw. Push it into the end of a second straw.

3. Repeat steps 1 and 2 to connect two other straws together.

4. Set the connected straws aside. They will make up the bridge frame.

5. Make a mark 2½ inches (6 cm) from the end of a new straw. Cut the straw at the mark.

6. Repeat step 5 until the remaining straws are cut into 2½-inch (6 cm) pieces.

Continued on the next page.

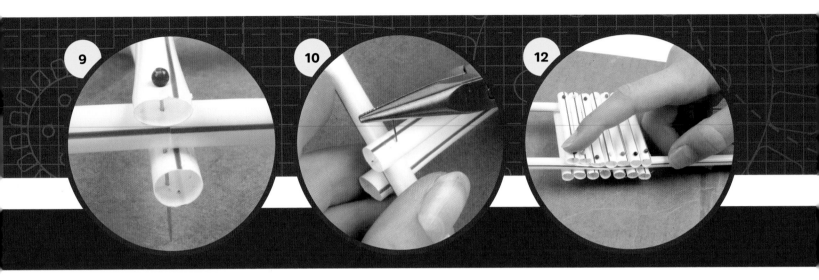

BENDY BEAM BRIDGE (CONTINUED)

⑦ Lay the sides of the bridge frame next to each other. Place them 2 inches (5 cm) apart. Make sure the ends line up.

⑧ Place a short straw across the bridge frame about 2 inches (5 cm) from one end. Place a second short straw underneath the frame.

⑨ Carefully push a pin through all three straws.

⑩ Use the pliers to bend the sharp end of the pin. This will hold the pin in place.

⑪ Repeat steps 9 and 10 to connect the other end of the short straws to the frame.

⑫ Add more short straws to the bridge. Place them side by side. Stop adding straws about 2 inches (5 cm) from the other end.

⑬ Lay the bridge across the tissue boxes. Place the cup on the bridge. Add marbles to the cup one by one. How many marbles can your bridge hold?

DIGGING DEEPER

There are two types of beam bridges. They are simply supported and continuous span. A simply supported bridge has one span. Its only supports are the abutments at each end. The longer the span, the weaker the bridge will be. So, simply supported bridges are best for short distances. Continuous span bridges have multiple short spans supported by piers. So, continuous span bridges can be longer overall.

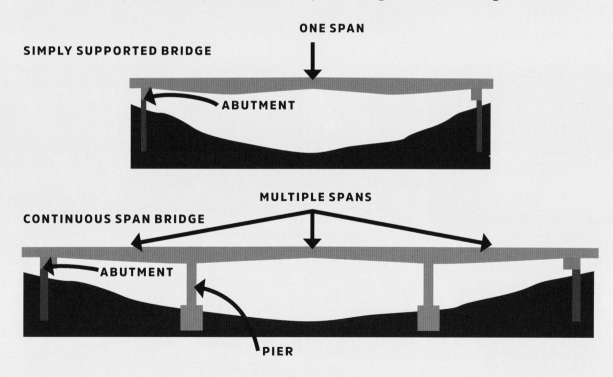

PAPER TRUSS
BRIDGE

MATERIALS: 38 small paper clips, 19 drinking straws

A truss is a structure made of beams arranged in triangles. Trusses are often used to strengthen bridges. Trusses allow bridges to support heavier loads.

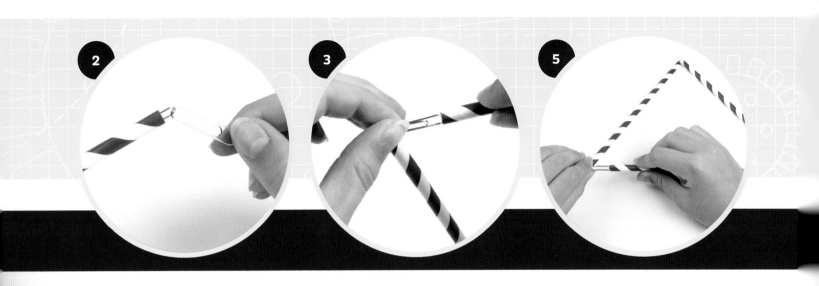

① Hook the smaller ends of two paper clips together.

② Push the wide end of one paper clip into the end of a straw.

③ Push the wide end of the other paper clip into the end of a second straw.

④ Hook two more paper clips together. Use them to add a third straw.

⑤ Hook two more paper clips together. Use them to connect the ends of the straws. The three straws should form a triangle.

⑥ Repeat steps 1 through 5 to make a second triangle. Lay the triangles side by side.

Continued on the next page.

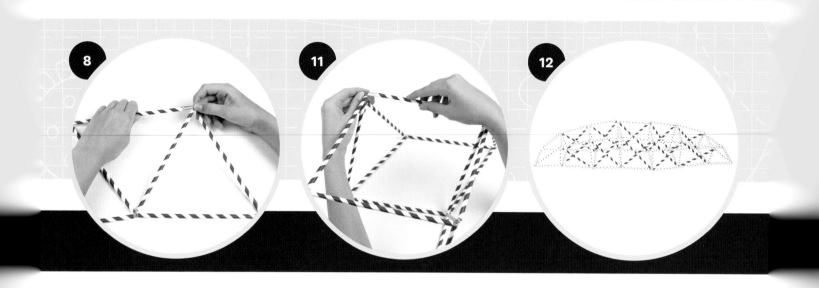

PAPER TRUSS BRIDGE (CONTINUED)

⑦ Pull a paper clip out of one of the bottom straws. Hook it to a paper clip in a bottom corner of the other triangle. Then push the paper clip back into the straw you pulled it out of. This connects the triangles at the bottom.

❽ Hook a paper clip to the top corner of each triangle. Push the wide end of each paper clip into the end of a new straw. This is one side of the truss bridge.

⑨ Repeat steps 1 through 8 to make the second side.

⑩ Hook a paper clip to each of the five joints in each side.

⓫ Use straws to connect the sides at the joints.

⓬ Now pull it apart and make a new truss bridge. Try using more straws or shorter straws. Get creative!

DIGGING DEEPER

The trusses on a truss bridge help carry the load! This is because a triangle is a strong shape. Weight applied to one point of a triangle is directed to its wider base. A truss has rows of many connected triangles. The weight of the bridge is spread throughout the truss. The truss can be above or below the bridge deck. Either way, it makes the bridge stronger.

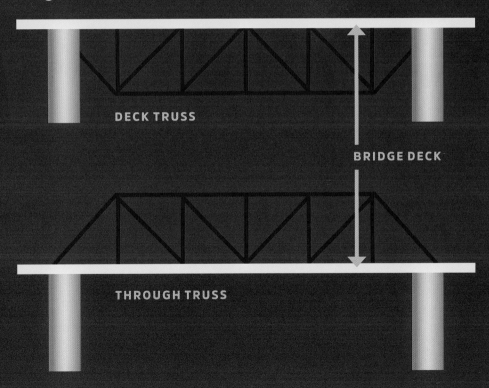

DECK TRUSS

BRIDGE DECK

THROUGH TRUSS

CLAY BRIDGE
CHALLENGE

MATERIALS: clay, cardboard, small tin box, pennies

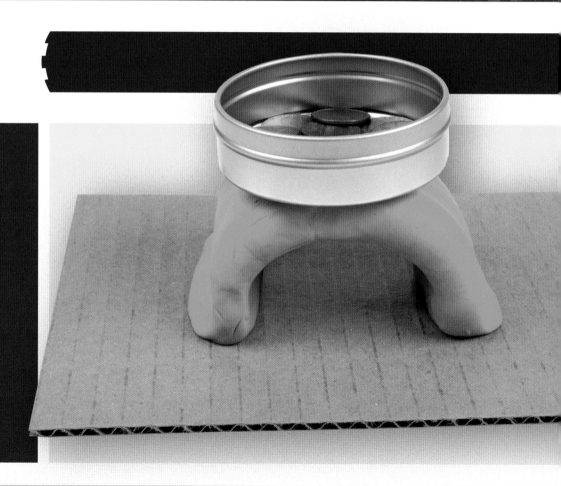

People have been making bridges for thousands of years. Early bridge builders had to figure out ways to make their bridges strong enough. Some bridges were weak and later **collapsed**. But many others are still standing!

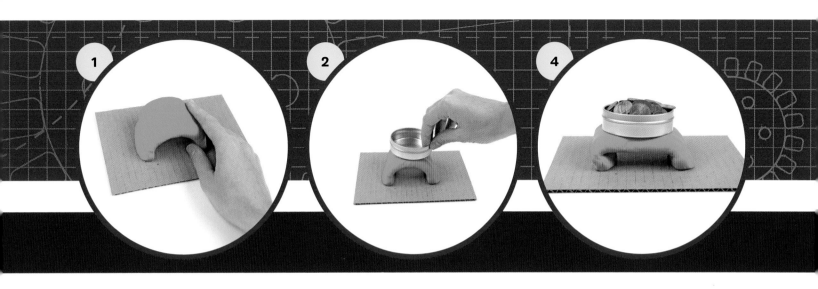

1 Mold clay into a bridge shape. Press the bottom onto the cardboard. Do not let the clay dry.

2 Place the tin box on the bridge.

3 Put pennies in the tin one at a time. See how many the bridge can hold.

4 Watch how the bridge sags and **collapses**.

5 Think about ways to make a stronger clay bridge. Try a different shape. Or make part of the bridge thicker or thinner. See what works best!

CONCLUSION

Bridges are important structures. If they are built correctly, bridges can last for hundreds, or even thousands, of years. Engineers work hard to create bridges that will help people move around easily and safely.

QUIZ

1. What is the surface of a bridge called?

2. Where is the Golden Gate Bridge?

3. There are ten main types of bridges.
   TRUE OR FALSE?

LEARN MORE ABOUT IT!

You can find out more about bridges all over the world at the library.
Or you can ask an adult to help you **research** bridges **online**.

Answers: 1. Bridge deck 2. California 3. False

GLOSSARY

collapse – to break apart and fall down.

mainland – the main part of a continent.

obstacle – something that you have to go over or around.

online – connected to the Internet.

pedestrian – a person who is walking.

research – to find out more about something.

slit – a narrow cut or opening.

traffic – the cars, trucks, pedestrians, ships, or planes moving along a route.

transfer – to pass from one thing or place to another.